The Fire Eater

The Fire Eater

POEMS

Jose Hernandez Diaz

Texas Review Press • Huntsville

Library of Congress Cataloging in Publication Data
is on file at the Library of Congress, Washington, DC

Cover photo courtesy of Aleksey Suvorov / Alamy Stock Photo

For my parents,
Maria and Esteban Hernández

Table of Contents

PART I

The Fire Eater

A fire eater performed his tricks on Hollywood Blvd by the entrance to the 101 Freeway. It was autumn. Just as he was about to inhale the bright flame, however, he slipped on a leaf and fell into the street. A motorcycle swerved out of the way and barely missed him. The fire eater quickly got up and jumped back onto the curb. He counted his lucky stars. One star. Two stars. Three stars. But there was no reason to go on. At least he felt that way at the moment. His family of circus performers had abandoned him. He would have to make it on his own. Perhaps he could go back to school? Who was he kidding? Eating fire was his only skill. It wasn't much of a marketable skill, either. Maybe he could make it on America's Got Talent? Or get hired in a Vegas show? These were his hopes and dreams. But were they merely pipe dreams? For now, at least, he would have to be content with eating fire on Hollywood Blvd by the 101 Freeway. Maybe someone important would discover him there, tomorrow. Maybe the flame would no longer scar his autumnal heart.

The Fire

A man woke up in a burning building. He ran to the front door. It was jammed. Then he threw a chair through the window. It shattered and glass fell everywhere. He was careful as he climbed out of the window. It was a three-story building. A preacher was down at the bottom, waiting to catch him. He jumped into the preacher's arms. On impact, they both transformed into pigeons. They flew away from the fire. Far away from the fire.

The Flame

A flame rode a skateboard to the corner liquor store. It bought a pack of Marlboro Lights. It packed the smokes and ignited a cigarette on its forehead. It inhaled the smoke. The flame rode a skateboard down Beach Blvd. It did tricks on the board. It saw a lady-flame leave Target and asked for her phone number. The flame was denied. It continued on the board, all the way to Pacific Coast Highway. It began to rain. The flame pondered the redundancy of rain. Suddenly, it fell off the board, and scattered into ash. The flame was no longer a flame. No longer aflame. A flame. Flame.

The Man and the Antlers

A man picked wild berries in the forest, ate them, and suddenly grew antlers. He was shocked. He ran around in circles, Why? Why? Then he saw a small creek. He looked into the water; he saw his antlers in the reflection, strong and sharp. Why me? He said. Why me? Then a bear approached him. He was startled for a moment, but then charged at the bear with force.

The Man and the Leaves

A man chased leaves down an urban street. The leaves moved fast. He ran and ran. A young boy stopped him, "Sir, why are you chasing leaves?" "I'm a starving artist, I haven't eaten in days!" the man said. "Have some oatmeal cookies," the boy said. "I only eat leaves!" the man said, running down the street. "I only eat leaves!"

The Man and the Sand Castle

A man sat at the beach and built a mighty sand castle. First, he built a giant watch tower. Then he built a sturdy bailey to guard the castle. Next, he built the various intricate rooms of the castle. Later, he dragged his fingers in the sand and made a river, just outside the castle doors. When he finished building the castle and river, he began to form an army of mud men and mud horses.

The Saxophonist

A man played a saxophone in the moonlight in the middle of the city. It was just turning into spring. He walked toward a traffic light. He briefly looked up at the tall buildings. A cab drove by and honked. The taxi driver waved at the man with the saxophone. He waved back, tipped his hat to an elderly woman, and then continued to play. The light turned green. He crossed the street. He walked around the artificial lake in the city. Joggers and walkers passed by and nodded their heads to the music. The man with the saxophone sat by the lake on a bench. He played "Locomotive" by Thelonious Monk. A lady and child came up to him and offered him a ten-dollar tip. The man collected the money into his beret. A raft of ducks swam in the artificial lake. At midnight, he finished playing, and walked back to his apartment.

Taxi to the Beach

A man hailed a taxi outside of his apartment. He was going to the beach. Suddenly, his fedora caught on fire from his cigarette. He fanned it outside the taxi window. Then his phone rang. It was the President of Mars. "Mr. Lopez, we need your vote next week. Can we count on you?" the President asked. "My hat is on fire!" Mr. Lopez shouted. "I'm sorry to hear that, Mr. Lopez, we'll send you a new one," the President of Mars said. "Thanks, Mr. President, but I can't vote for you," Mr. Lopez said. "Then you don't get a hat. That's how it works. Goodbye!" the President said. Mr. Lopez hung-up and tossed the flaming fedora out of the window. "To the beach!" he shouted.

The Longboard

A man rode a longboard in Downtown Los Angeles. It was overcast in the city. He listened to Gary Clark Jr on his headphones as he rode. He wore his favorite Dodgers jersey. He was not going anywhere specifically; he just liked riding his longboard in the city. He rode through the USC campus. He smoked a cigarette. The Metro howled in the distance. He saw a few seagulls overhead. As Gary Clark Jr played a hypnotic guitar into his ear, he felt as if he were flying and everything were okay. Nothing could stop him now.

The Red House

The red house has five windows. The red house does not have any new clocks. The red house has three Rottweilers, all of them named Samuel. The red house has quiet afternoons, despite all the furniture. The red house has bougainvillea running along a brick wall. The red house has a blue fire pit. The red house has seven candles instead of lamps. The red house was never yours. The red house has a lime interior. The red house has two roosters and an ant problem. The red house never forgives. The red house is not painted red. The red house has three orange trees in the backyard. The red house is not for sale. The red house doesn't write during holidays. The red house has doors as mirrors. The red house, pale and drunk, at night.

The Target

A man aimed his rifle at a poorly painted target on the trunk of a willow tree. The target was of a smiling clown, standing in profile and waving. The man aimed for the clown's nose. He missed. He then aimed for the clown's heart. Another miss. He was down to his final shot. The man aimed his rifle at the clown's predictably large shoe. He fired and hit the clown right in the big toe. The clown let out a violent cry, "I'm hit! I'm hit!" In utter shock, the man threw down his rifle and sprinted in the opposite direction. He searched for his canoe amid tall swamp grasses. When he finally found it, he jumped inside and pedaled for his life. Later, he turned around and saw the clown limping toward the water, with a machete in hand. The man put his head down and didn't stop pedaling until he reached the small town. When he finally saw the locals gathered in the town square that summer night, he never felt a greater joy.

The Field of Marigolds

A man woke up in a field of marigolds. He had no idea how he'd gotten there. He jumped to his feet and wiped the dirt from his brow. He looked around at thousands of flowers. It reminded him of autumn. And pumpkins. It was autumn, in fact. He smelled the bitter flower and immediately pulled away. He jumped on his bike and rode away from the marigolds. Upon leaving, he didn't take a photo of the flowers because he wanted to paint them fresh from memory.

Sunflowers in the City

A man fell asleep on the subway. He woke up in another city. When he got off the train, it began to rain sunflowers. It was the middle of winter. He lit a cigarette and walked to a park. He sat on a graffitied bench and wrote a poem. The poem was about sunflowers, winter, and the city. He went to the library and submitted the poem to various literary magazines. He titled it, 'Sunflowers in the City.'

The Rose Bush

A man plucked an orange rose from a bush, smelled it, and then burst into flames. The flames eventually died out. Ash. Later, the man's daughter came looking for him. All she found were scattered ashes. The girl then walked up to the bush, picked a blue rose, and smelled it. She quickly turned into water and splashed to the floor. She washed away the ash.

The Mime and the Old Man

A mime fell to the floor and pretended he was dead. A young couple walked by. They stared and pointed but continued on their way. Then a butcher walked by. He tugged on the mime's sleeve. After no response, he too continued on his way. Then an old man walked by. He clapped his hands beside the mime's ear. No response. Then he shouted into his ear. Nothing. Finally, the old man lay on the floor, with the mime, and pretended he was dead.

The Mime and the Music

A mime took a boombox to a small park in the city. He pressed play. He pretended to open up a case and take out a saxophone. He mimed to play. He closed his eyes and swayed his head back-and-forth. The small crowd cheered. He nodded at them to show his appreciation. Then he mimed to put the saxophone back in its case. All of this in time with the boombox. Next, he faked to take out another case, this time for a guitar. He mimed to tune it up. Then he pretended to play on his knee, very passionately. The crowd cheered some more. Finally, he mimed to take out a harmonica and pretended to play. He moved his fingers by his mouth and tapped his foot on the floor. The crowd was very pleased with all of his performances. Plenty of people tipped money into his top hat. It was a matter of respect.

The Moon

A man woke up on the surface of the moon. He didn't float away. He sat on the pale floor. He pulled out a cigarette and took a drag. He saw the earth in the distance. It looked like a blue and green tennis ball, only significantly larger. He remembered his childhood in California. How he wanted to be an astronaut when he grew up. Nothing could stop him now.

How Far Is the Moon?

A man played an acoustic guitar on the surface of the moon. He didn't float away. He looked at the earth in the distance. It reminded him of his family in California; nostalgia. Then he looked at the stars.

Next, he played a song he'd written. It was called, "How Far Is the Moon?" It was about his experience on the moon but also autumn. When he finished playing, he took out a cigarette and took a drag. Only one thought remained: none of the stars are the same.

The Dragon and the Coyote

A man looked into a mirror, but he didn't recognize himself. Instead, he saw a dragon and a coyote engaged in a game of chess. The dragon moved first: middle pawn, two spaces. Then the coyote parroted the move. They stared into each other's eyes. Neither budged.

After three hours, they called it a draw. The dragon flapped its scarlet wings, and flew toward a nearby mountain. The coyote began to howl a lullaby. When the man eventually stopped looking into the mirror, he realized he's the dragon. And he's the coyote. It's always been that way.

The Beautiful Bird

A man played an acoustic guitar on a deserted island. He sang a song about seagulls. It was called "The Beautiful Bird." He played his guitar and sang various songs until the moon came up. Then he built a fire. He slept beneath a palm tree.

He had a dream about the ocean. He was on a sailboat in the dream. He saw a pod of dolphins. They swam beside the boat. He didn't know where he was going, but he was traveling at a fast pace. The dolphins guided him toward an island. The wind was cold on his face. When he landed ashore, he found a seagull skeleton on the sand. He picked up the bird's skull and examined it. Written on the back of the skull were the words "the beautiful bird." The man collected the delicate bones and gave them a proper burial. After he had placed the last sand on the tomb of the bird, he sang the requisite song.

The Mountain Man

A man drove his truck away from his suburban hometown. He wanted to see the mountains. He drove for two hours. It was snowing on the road. He'd lent his snow tire chains to his friend the week before, so he stopped his car when it got too icy. He got out and started skiing. Luckily, he'd brought his skis. He climbed the mountain on his skis. It wasn't even that difficult for him. He was a natural. When he got to the top of the mountain, he shouted: "Hooray! I have climbed the mountain of fear! I have defeated the mountain and all her might!"

Then he started to build a fire. He roasted some chicken and vegetables. When he finished eating, he started to write a letter to his 5th grade teacher, Mrs. Cranford. The letter began: Dear Mrs. Cranford, Thank you for all your kindness and support. You taught me so much. Maybe the most important lesson being that of respect for others. I am forever grateful for your guidance. Sincerely, The Mountain Man. He put the letter in his pocket and started heading back home. He made it home and went to bed. The next day he sent the letter to his teacher, along with a copy of his celebrated book of photography. The photos in the book were black-and-white shots of Downtown Los Angeles. He signed the book: Respectfully, your student, The Mountain Man.

The Abandoned Shore

A man woke up on an abandoned shore. He had no idea where he was. There weren't any people around; only seagulls, sand, and ocean. He picked up a sand dollar and threw it into the ocean. Then he took off his shirt and jumped in the water. It was very cold, but it didn't bother him.

Then he saw a ship on the horizon. It had a pirate-skull flag and cannons. The man quickly exited the water and put on his clothes. He ran as fast as possible, away from the beach. When he finally stopped running, he was in the middle of a large city. He was elated to hear the sounds of traffic. Immediately, he fell asleep at a bus stop, in the middle of the city.

PART II

The Astronaut

A man in a Pink Floyd shirt woke up on his living room couch. There was a party going on in the house. The man in the Pink Floyd shirt didn't recognize anyone at the party. He wasn't drunk. He tapped a man in a green sweater's shoulder, "Hello, who are you?" he asked. "I'm Gary," he said. "Yes, but what are you all doing here?" the man in the Pink Floyd shirt asked. "We are celebrating your graduation from Astronaut training, of course," the man in the green sweater said. "Of course," the man in a Pink Floyd shirt said. He didn't actually recall being an Astronaut. In fact, he hated math and science. Was more of an arts and crafts guy. Besides, he had an incredible fear of heights. The next thing he knew, the guests were handing out glasses for champagne and a toast. They started chanting, "Speech! Speech!"

The man in a Pink Floyd shirt grabbed a glass of champagne and stood in front of the eager crowd. He raised his glass, cleared his throat, and spoke, "I'd like to thank you all for coming tonight. I'm honored by your presence. I've wanted to be an astronaut since I was a little boy growing up in the mountains of Arizona. I used to dream about existence beyond the clouds. Now my dreams are coming true. Reach for the stars, friends. Never let fear defeat you. Cheers to space! Cheers to all of you!" he said. The crowd erupted in cheer and they clinked their glasses together. They had long conversations until after midnight when they began to disperse. After everyone was gone, the man in a Pink Floyd shirt went to sleep and dreamt about another world's dawn. Another galaxy, even.

The Balloon and the Helicopter

A man in a Pink Floyd shirt sat by a window. He saw a balloon rise and rise. The balloon crashed into a helicopter. The helicopter sliced the balloon into countless pieces. The man in a Pink Floyd shirt laughed and laughed. It began to rain. The man in a Pink Floyd shirt pulled a book from the shelf. The book was called, The Balloon and the Helicopter. He opened the book, closed it, and went to the kitchen to make coffee. He couldn't find coffee, so he decided to go to the store. When he opened the door, he found hundreds if not thousands of pieces of balloon on the front porch. The man in a Pink Floyd shirt laughed and laughed. What a day, he said to himself. What a day? He returned to the window and gazed away, looking for another balloon. Then the man in a Pink Floyd shirt thought of coffee again and returned to the kitchen. Oh yes, he said. I need to go to the store for coffee. What a day, the man in a Pink Floyd shirt said. What a day?

Train Out of Town

A man in a Pink Floyd shirt planned to ride the subway to the city. He wanted to get away from his suburban hometown. He packed a lunch, cigarettes, and a pair of sunglasses. When he arrived on the train, it was mostly empty.

He rode the train all the way downtown and watched as it filled with passengers. He looked up at the tall buildings and heard a blues guitar playing in the background. On the window, he noticed his reflection juxtaposed with the city. When he arrived at his stop, a crowd gathered to enter and exit the train. The man in a Pink Floyd shirt maneuvered through the crowd and rode the escalator to the downtown exit: the city.

The Flowing Circles

A man in a Pink Floyd shirt taught himself to play the harmonica. He played beside a river, next to the mountains. A prominent waterfall splashed in the background. The man developed into an expert harmonica player. He signed a contract with an obscure yet refined record company. The man in a Pink Floyd shirt eventually went on tour with a band. They called themselves, The Flowing Circles. The Flowing Circles, or The Circles as they were affectionately called, toured Europe and Latin America. When they finally returned to America, they took a domestic vacation. They bought dark sun glasses and rode bicycles by the ocean. When the time came to write their next album, they retreated back to the mountains, by the river and waterfall.

The Hole

A man in a Pink Floyd shirt dug a giant hole in his backyard. Someone had told him to go to hell earlier that day. Assuming hell to be beneath the soil, the man in a Pink Floyd shirt picked up a shovel, and got to work. The person who told him to go to hell was a professional juggler. He juggled axes, bowling pins, and soccer balls. The man in a Pink Floyd shirt had accidentally bumped into him causing him to drop his soccer balls. That's when he told him to go to hell. The man in a Pink Floyd shirt dug and dug. He told himself when he got to hell, he would fistfight Lucifer. He didn't much like his chances against Lucifer, but he thought it a noble endeavor. Finally, at midnight, the man in a Pink Floyd shirt dropped his shovel from fatigue, and fell asleep inside the hole. When he woke up the next day, he no longer wanted to dig a hole to hell. He just wanted black coffee. Black coffee with toast and eggs. Bon appétit, man in a Pink Floyd shirt.

The Piñata

A man in a Pink Floyd shirt fell from a tall ladder. He had been trying to hang a piñata from his roof to a nearby tree. The man was celebrating his 30th birthday. His friend ran to his side, "Are you okay?" "I'm fine," he said. "Let's just forget about the piñata," his friend said. "Nonsense," the man in a Pink Floyd shirt said. "Birthdays aren't memorable without smashing piñatas." The man in a Pink Floyd shirt climbed the ladder again, this time his friend held it steady. When he got to the top, he called for the piñata. It was a large, colorful piñata of a rooster. After a couple tries, they managed to hang the piñata from the roof to the tree. The man rocked a broken broom stick back-and-forth in his sweaty palms. Then he began smashing the rooster-piñata. Eventually, turquoise beads fell from the smashed piñata. Everyone ran to collect the fine beads. The man in a Pink Floyd shirt felt tremendous joy. He was no longer in his twenties. Then everyone went inside to eat cake and drink craft beer. Happy birthday, man in a Pink Floyd shirt.

The United States of the Moon

A man in a Pink Floyd shirt fell asleep on a rocking chair on the moon. He had a dream about the government. The government gave him a salary of $235,000 per year because he was a famous astronaut. He was building a civilization on the moon. The nation was going to be called The United States of the Moon. His chair was still rocking as he slept. Fifteen of his fellow astronauts had come with him to start a civilization on the moon. They were from various Earth countries, including, Mexico, Japan, and Australia. None of the astronauts were very good at poker. One of them was a saint. The rest were common astronauts.

Then a moonquake happened. The man in a Pink Floyd shirt jumped out of his rocking chair. He bounced around the moon. It shook for an hour. When it was over, all that survived were the space ship and the man in a Pink Floyd shirt. He boarded the space ship with tears in his eyes. He flew toward Earth, wounded, but not defeated.

The Guitarist

A man in a Pink Floyd shirt threw a football toward the top of a skyscraper, in Downtown Los Angeles. He was trying to prove a point to his girlfriend. He told her he could throw a football as high as a skyscraper. The girlfriend thought he was crazy but followed him downtown anyway. The man in a Pink Floyd shirt was just trying to impress her. He thought she was the type who would be impressed by a strong arm. After his failed throw, the girlfriend explained to him, just be yourself. Then they lived happily ever after. That is, until he lost his job at the rocking chair factory. He worked hard with his hands, building rocking chairs. He wasn't exactly proud of his work, but work is work. The man in a Pink Floyd shirt was fired because he refused to put on his uniform one day. "Take off that Pink Floyd shirt!" his boss said. "I refuse!" the man in a Pink Floyd shirt said. He was fired right around the holidays. Then his girlfriend broke up with him. He now plays a mean guitar. Rest in peace, man in a Pink Floyd shirt.

The Skeleton at Bat

A man in a Pink Floyd shirt plucked an azalea from a garden. It was the beginning of spring. The sun was shining, nicely. He thought about how happy he was he hadn't smoked a cigarette in three weeks. He took a deep breath. He drank some water. He decided to take the azalea to his girlfriend. She said, "Thank you for the beautiful flower!" They embraced. Then he went home and painted for three hours. He drank coffee. But his paintings were not flowery at all. They were rather dark. But it brought him peace. He fell asleep after he painted a skeleton smoking a cigarette beneath the moonlight.

When the man in a Pink Floyd shirt woke up the next day, he rode his longboard to the Venice Boardwalk. He sold his painting for $150. He considered it a successful day. He went home and ate and then watched the Dodger game. Later, when he finished watching the game, he decided to paint a skeleton with a Dodgers jersey, swinging a bat at Dodger Stadium under the lights. He called it, "The Skeleton at Bat." The next day he sold it for another $150. It was turning into a very productive week, indeed. He loved spring. And skeletons. And the moon. And the Dodgers.

PART III

The Skeleton and the Book

A skeleton sat by a lake and read a book. The book was about the origins of the Land of Skeletons. The Land of Skeletons was founded six hundred years ago. The skeletons rose from the grave and demanded their freedom. Long had they waited in the cold earth. The skeletons fought many dragons in order to gain their freedom. Many rode valiant horses to fight their enemy.

When the war was over, the skeletons raised their revered flag: a skeleton and a sword. They began to build a civilization of skeletons. They elected officials. They danced in nightclubs. They surfed in the ocean. War never returned to the Land of Skeletons. They lived in peace with the crows, mountain goats, and the redwoods alike. The Land of the Skeletons is our home.

The Skeleton at the Park

A skeleton walked in the park in spring. It walked up to a rose bush and smelled a white rose. It sat down by the bush and started to draw what it saw. It drew a woman's skeleton walking a Chihuahua. Then it drew a man's skeleton with an ice cream cart selling popsicles to some kid skeletons. It drew a group of skeletons playing basketball in the mild sun. When the skeleton finished the drawing, it titled it, "The Skeleton at the Park." Then it went home and ate dinner: beef stew. The next day the skeleton rode his bicycle to the city and sold the drawing for $100. It was enough to pay the phone bill and buy a pack of cigarettes. It was a productive weekend.

The Skeleton at the Pier

A skeleton walked on a pier holding a balloon. It was a mild Sunday; 75 degrees. The balloon had a drawing of a shark on a surfboard. The skeleton sat down on a bench and stared at the waves. Plenty of seagulls flew overhead. Some seagulls landed on the pier looking for food. The skeleton smoked a cigarette. Then it walked to the edge of the pier just as the sun was setting. The skeleton took a photo of the sunset and posted it on Instagram. It loved living on the west coast. When it started to get dark, the skeleton headed back home on a black bicycle. It tied the balloon onto the bike frame as it rode in the moonlight.

The Skeleton with the Sunglasses

A skeleton rode a bicycle in the city. It was the beginning of summer. He had on a pair of black sunglasses. He was going to the library downtown. It was his first month cigarette-free. He hadn't had a drink in a month, either, but he still planned on eventually having the occasional celebratory drink. The skeleton rode by the old gothic church. The pointed arches and crosses were beautiful to him, even though he's not religious. He took a photo of the church with his phone. Then he rode by the bowling alley. It looked like it was from the 1970's, but it was still going strong. The skeleton took another photo. Then he arrived at the library. He went straight to the computer section and wrote a story.

It was called, "The Skeleton with the Sunglasses." It's a slice of life story about a skeleton graffiti artist who rides a longboard with sunglasses in the city. He submits the story to various literary magazines, including, Parrot Skull Review, Bones Literary Journal, and Death by Roses Quarterly. It's accepted in three months at Death by Roses Quarterly. The skeleton celebrates by having a bottle of champagne. He parties until 2 a.m. with his skeleton writer friends. Eccentric types. Then he goes to bed and dreams about the federal government. Buenas noches, Don Esqueleto.

The Skeleton and the Skateboard

A skeleton rode a skateboard in a city park. He was on his way home from work. He works at a library downtown as a security guard. Earlier that day, a ghost stole a book of Shakespearean Sonnets. The skeleton chased the ghost out of the library. The ghost jumped on a scooter and rode away. The skeleton wagged his finger at the ghost and said, "Don't ever come back! That was my favorite book!"

As the skeleton rode his skateboard through the park, it started to rain. The skeleton put on his hood and rode carefully through the damp streets. He saw a bus drive by. It had a movie advertisement on the side of the bus. The movie was called "The Shark of the Night." The skeleton was fascinated by the advertisement. When he got home, he called his skeleton friend, Bones Garcia, and they went to the movies to watch the film. It was scary but thrilling and they enjoyed themselves, immensely. The following day was Sunday. The skeleton stayed home and watched baseball all day. Nothing bothered him. He drank green tea and rested for the long week ahead.

The Skeleton and the Guitar

A skeleton played an acoustic guitar by a lake. It sang folk songs and patriotic songs. People passed by and placed coins and bills inside the skeleton's hat. Koi fish swam in the lake beside the skeleton. At sunset, the skeleton played one final song. It was written by the skeleton. It was called "The Skeleton and the Guitar." The crowd cheered at the end of the song. As the cheers faded, the skeleton collected its belongings, and rode its horse home to the edge of the city.

The Skeleton and the Piano

A skeleton played a piano in the middle of a cemetery. It was Christmas Eve. He played "Nocturnes" by Chopin. It was a misty night. The skeleton sat deep in thought. His mother had taught him how to play when he was a young skeleton. She'd been deceased for a century. A crow landed on the piano as he played. The skeleton smiled at it. The bright moon floated above the sporadic clouds. The skeleton wore a scarf and a fedora. When he finished playing, at midnight, he smoked a cigarette by a creek. He wondered where the time had gone. After his last puff of smoke, he got on his motorcycle and rode to his house in the southeast suburbs of Los Angeles.

Acknowledgments

Grateful acknowledgment is made to the following literary magazines where some of these poems first appeared, sometimes in different forms:

The American Poetry Review
The Awl
Bat City Review
Bennington Review
The Cincinnati Review
The Cortland Review
Diode Poetry Journal
Empty Mirror
Guesthouse
Hobart
Hotel Amerika
The Journal
The Iowa Review
New Delta Review
New Orleans Review
North American Review
Pidgeonholes
Pleiades
Poetry Northwest
Vinyl